Origin Myths

'I hear the father of the ancient men.'
WILLIAM BLAKE

'What I best see I see ill.'
SAMUEL BECKETT

Duncan Wu

Origin Myths

Shearsman Books

First published in the United Kingdom in 2024 by
Shearsman Books Ltd
PO Box 4239
Swindon
SN3 9FN

Shearsman Books Ltd Registered Office
30–31 St. James Place, Mangotsfield, Bristol BS16 9JB
(this address not for correspondence)

www.shearsman.com

ISBN 978-1-84861-940-1

ACKNOWLEDGEMENTS
The following poems have appeared elsewhere:

Acumen: 'Fired Up'; *Cutthroat*: 'Blood Memory' and 'Origin Myth';
The Georgia Review: 'Foxed' (as 'Vulpine Magic') and 'Orthoptera
Chorale'; *The London Magazine*: 'Cleansed' and 'Backcountry'
(as 'Secret'); *The New Criterion*: 'Roof Repair'; *Notre Dame Review*:
'Insectisonic' (as 'Facing the Music'); *The Oxford Magazine*: 'Now',
'Psychic Bobcat', 'Skin'; *Raritan*: 'Melville's Crossing'. *Sierra Nevada
Review*: 'Cabin'; *Temenos Annual Review*: 'Constellation' and
'Healing Blue'.

Contents

For Dean Brodrick

and i.m. Michael Searson (1960–1980)

Land of goldenrod, nocturnal cicadas,
arrowhead ferns, snakeroot, ghosts, kraken,
the heavy freight of grief in landscape.

Origin Myth

Ice flying upward, straight to the face, scalding,
blistering, blinding—for thousands of miles their
dogs hauled their lives from world to world to where
they found their ancestral dreamsite, halting

here, at this stream supplied by mountain springs.
I live here now but this hill remains their own
where once they raised livestock, carved bluestone,
ploughed the earth, cured animal skins.

At dawn, I go down to the creek to bathe
where, around this time, the tribe would come
to cleanse the spirit in the rising sun,
encouraged by love of this spot to brave

the ice-fresh water coursing through the creek.
I feel them here in the house of light,
in rocks and stones, the skirling heights
of these ancient trees, in the bluejay's shriek.

In the Potomac, I slice through the river's skin,
dive down, submerge myself in its flow,
find the place where thought begins to slow
and restlessness of the mind goes still.

Blood-Memory

The tribe lives on in the earth they tilled
and the trees they planted, from which my shack
long ago was built. Tell me whose attack
destroyed the world, what armed militia willed
them from their ancestral lands. The earth
remembers and, if it could, would repay
the heavy tax exacted that bleak day
and return to them this blackened turf.
Blood calls out to blood, appeals to brain and heart
and guts with feeling deep as love,
deep as first love, wild with all regret; above,
the sky calls out for justice, but in vain—
despite its crazed distempered rage
at knowing nothing can be made to change.

Resurrection Water

Blood-darkness of this forest is physical,
pulls you in and draws you deeper in,
demanding you forget the self, begin
to pass through barriers super-mystical.
In rub of stone and hoof you may detect,
from miles beneath, the tremor of lava
flooding into a spitting Niagara,
ancient source of water that once leapt
through Eden—Pishon, Gihon, Tigris
and Euphrates—sublimed through alchemic
vessels, now discharged into hydroptick
channels such as Scotts Run Creek, which blitzes
the perceiving mind, summons all that's fled
and restores to sight the angry, vengeful dead.

Dakota

Tribal elders knew these trails were spirit-
charged, invested with occult energy
that could ease the journey between the worlds.
I knew nothing of that when I arrived,
but I loved the half-hour stroll to the mailbox
even when no mail was to be found—
walking the trail put me in touch with those
who laid it. One afternoon I climbed the ridge
and headed out. Though it was late I thought,
if quick, I could be back by sundown.
Clumps of butterfly milkweed straggled along
the track to greet the passer-by. I knelt,
plucked the petals from a plant, tasted, spat it out:
bitterer far from what I'd thought. The light
was fading fast but I slowed down to inspect
Virginia bluebells, spring beauties and
birdfoot violets, as they quivered gently
in the evening breeze. I was dawdling and
picked up my pace, running the last quarter mile.
By the time I reached the box the sky was dark;
there was nothing inside, as was so often
the case. I slammed it shut, began the slow
walk back. This was the time when bloodsuckers
of the night started to go primal and
here I was—yet I quickened my pace.
Ten minutes in, the path had vanished, though
I pushed on, all bearings trashed, hoping
to find my way—but didn't, couldn't, and
the more I walked, the darker it got till

I was tripping on the stress-chems. "Hello!"
called a voice far out in the black, a male voice.
Could he see me? At first I saw nothing,
then, peering far in the distance, made out
a dark-haired, dark-skinned man and boy. "Hello!",
I shouted, "Do you know the way to the cabin
beneath the ridge?" A pause, then the man called,
"This is Dakota. From now on, she takes you home."
Only then did I notice the dog.
They spoke to it, the boy hugged it, then sent
it toward me. As she cantered across
the leaf-strewn ground, I saw she had the build
of pit-bull, coat of malamute or husky,
friendly as you could wish. Nuzzling my hand,
she engaged my eyes. "She will guide you",
called the man. "Treat her well." I stroked the fur
on her back and when I looked up, man and boy
had gone. Dakota didn't wait, set out
into the bush and, as I followed, found
myself not running but falling, the trail
flying out into darkness, as if with the dog
I passed through vectors of force known only to her.
In no time I was back on the ridge—
glanced up to see flashes in the clouds—
and as we reached the cabin door the storm blew up.
I opened it and she leapt on the windowseat
as if the place were hers and hers had ever been.
That took me aback, I now being her guest,
not the other way round. I lit the fire
and settled down, by which time she was sleeping,
which she's doing as I write this now.
Her name means "friend" or "ally". She came

with those who lived here first, travelers from Asia
swathed in skins, faces weathered, for whom
she pulled supplies through worlds on worlds—
crossing deserts, arctic wastes, canyons of ice.
Spaced in, she maps the world with eyes wide open,
limbs fast-twitching, reconceives topography
of the real to make it ideal, to ease
tomorrow's journey, and if ever I forsake
this world for another, set foot beyond
the realm of the mailbox, she will be my guide.

Cabin

Three centuries since its frame was raised
using wood logged upon this site—oak, beech;
surfaces inside blackened with age, planed
by hands long stilled, hammered into place. Creaks
at every joint, footfalls, noises, knocks, but
its ghosts no longer frighten me—they're trapped
outside the window, their voices can't cut
through the glass. Its joints, though mostly inexact,
bespeak their maker, someone like me,
living rough upon this slope, crafting wood
with unpracticed but devoted skill. The
cabin is a barque upon the flood
ferrying its spectral crew tirelessly
through the years, a rough and turbulent sea.

Tribal Knowledge

I was a child when they spoke to me
of virtue abandoned, goodness chided,
dark clouds and storms coming in from the sea,
the deepening terror that all was blighted.
I struggled to see what it was they meant.
They kept returning, shadows and voices
at the edge of sleep when I thought I dreamt
they spoke of my grandmother—choices
she made when, armed, she fought in the streets in
the Canton coup. And again I see her,
sharp as a razor, haranguing
the crowds, vivid and true as I were there.
Now, in this primordial dark, far
from the world, she tells me, "Deeds are what you are."

Dirt Justice

Smeared on, this dirt's invisible,
transmitting power from the earth's deep center
that pulses through the invincible
heart of this land, released when some distemper
made Fairfax County erupt in tidal waves
of fiery dust hurled at the sky,
so forging Virginia's highlands, vales,
and coastal plains. I suspect that's why
this black mud fills both soul and veins, as if I'd
emerged out of this disputed ground,
seeded by a serpent's tooth. Beside
this creek, I tell the trees that history's brown
warriors burn lies, put myth to flight,
bring the world's injustices to light.

Now

This cabin stands on a hole in the hillside
where Confederate soldiers wintered out.
Legend has it after Lee surrendered
     one came back, a former scout,

built it, spent his last years within its walls.
Was it here you nursed your oldest friend to
premature death from a gangrenous wound?
     Did you feed him the local brew,

Mrs Swinks's moonshine, to kill the pain
and help him sleep? And at the last, did you
promise to take tokens of love to his
     parents and girl? That's when you knew

you'd come back to tend his grave—a promise
of his last minutes, and one you kept. See,
I'd love to consider this rustic spot
     the emblem of fidelity,

friendship raised in timber and stone, relic
of the freezing winter of '62,
but it's a shack, that's all, where I live now,
     what some call a room with a view

with no known history but this present time,
the only history a man can own:
a "now" on a sun-drenched day, me and dog
     Dakota, forever, alone.

Birth

Green shoots leap up in shady forests, born
of this black earth, uprisen at mid-noon;
 I hear their cries and see this calm lagoon
engorged with vernal energy, torn
from nowhere—nurtured by the tribe, planted
in this earth, and guarded now by me.
Landscape of love made of such beauty
as makes angels weep, its enchanted
walks unchanged since the day that they were laid.
It's a gateway to earth's original perfection
as it lives in human conception
in memories we're born with, by which we're made.
So when did we decide the first to kill?
And when nuke this goddamn joint to hell?

Promise

A man atop the nearest hill attached to
our valley, large as a god. He had to be
what remained of the first people—statue
of some mythic being. Yet when I climbed up the
hill I found nothing—no carving in stone
or wood. Though he hasn't returned since those
early times, I know he still walks upon
this ground—as if some bone in the skull chose
to make me hyper-aware of what this
valley witnessed. It makes me feel inward quiet
and respect for all who lived here once,
souls both peaceable and defiant.
Their voices at night make promises not demands:
one day they'll reclaim their ancestral lands.

Guardian

Dakota low-crouched, to say she meant no harm,
while round her gathered twenty adult deer;
on the patch of ground in front of her
two speckled fawns asleep, eyes closed, breathing
slow and slow. I held my breath, watched through
the window before stepping silently
into summer air. Darkness began to fall
yet the creatures declined to take their leave.
I remained on the porch, transfixed, then shut
my eyes while night swept through me like a breeze.
Before sun rises, light is fragile, wash
on porcelain; the cool dawn sun touched my
forehead as I blinked myself back into the world.
Dakota hadn't moved, alert as when
light began to fade. After a while the doe
rejoined us, watched the sleepers in their den,
then stepped forward to do what only she could—
nuzzled her babies into wakefulness.
The fawns stood mid the grasses, trailed their mother
down to the creek. Their sleep is a miracle,
an act of trust and love, passage to a
sacred place, old as the tribe, old as this forest.

Red Jasper

Etched, painted here by the creek, this way-
stone marks the point of rebirth
where the tribe came to shed sweat and earth
from their awakened bodies. Every day
I seek it out when I come to bathe myself:
irregular oval, salmon-tinted,
three feet wide, bedded where I found it.
I cleaned, dried it, brought it back to health.
It resides just where the water's fastest
as it flows between these banks, receiving
their virtues—smooth, sandy, worn, yet feeling
flesh-like, soft as lips the moment they're kissed.
So tell me why, if we must turn to dust,
such knowledge lacks power to redeem us?

Cutter's Dust

Energy in this mound of earth buzzes
where the tribe carved arrowheads, ax-heads,
obsidian, flint: fragments, flakes and shreds
rise to the light by obscure impulses
then submerge again, as if their tools
were still at work, defined by their frenzy,
complete immersion in an endless sea
of action. For an instant I see whose
shadow fell here, the flow of dust in slow
descent, filling this air, possessing beauty
beyond estimation—that of coolly
managed human touch, a passing thing, its flow,
the *chik-chak-chuk* of the cutter's prime utensil
transformed into something monumental.

At Rhita's Tomb

Day-of-judgment darkness at mid-noon;
a distant roar that says the weather's going
to break. I'm standing by the tree whose roots
are tight entwined as serpent-dreadlocks
of Medusa with the bank of Scotts Run creek.
I step forward in the murky air
thinking myself transparent as a ghost
seen from the gorge—spirit as it makes
its solitary way from one world to the next.
I turn back to the cabin and step inside
as sheets of storm-drift clatter on the roof,
sky low-swagging on the valley-floor,
drifting toward that tireless bloated beast—
Old Potomac. Sudden, back it comes:
forty years ago, heart of Cymru—
groundscratching clouds that drench and chill now force-feed
panic juice straight to the brain: apexed on
that titanic wall of ancient volcano,
blade of rock, site of druid sacrifice
on table rock, three thousand feet above
the world on that solitary wedge of
dolerite, I'm rock to face, hyper-
tuned in to the world's too-rapid revolutions,
manes of vapor coming in hot before
flying out into the sempiternal
void, again and yet again, making me
conceive I too might float into the nothing
that was and something that wasn't, where I'd
find that tribe who since I was four have helped

me recall what has not yet occurred—dervish
visions, designs etched in limestone by the
palaeolithic cave. Maggoty sheep,
some horned, grazed far below on hilly patches
where, since the time of Caractacus, they'd thrived,
eavesdropping on the clouds. The mountain coupled
its nerve-pulse to spine and heart and brains, though
the summit, barely fifty feet hence,
was forever beyond my reach. Engulfed
by blackest of all black clouds, hearing only
the wind's crazed mutterings, chilled to the withers,
I merged with that living monster the rock,
its freezing blood pulsing slow and slow—that
now, in my cabin, Jacobite-fired, thought-
traveling decades, a pulse shoots up
the spine, the mountain's summons, for I know
reason won't save me, nor the knowledge this
has been coming for years, and though in domestic
safety, I can't stop my knees from shaking,
crumpling, flesh on granite, hanging on that
ridge, looking at those sheep—beyond, the hooded,
all-consuming sea and at core some terror,
some ecstasy as I wait for what comes next.

Shimmer

Falling waters sing of life and death,
eclogue of the turning world. I approach
their familiar sound—cold reproach
of time lost, never to be regained. Breaths
that rise in lands of blue mist feed these streams—
now bright, now glistening, bristling with sunlight—
yet as I stand here something happens, despite
myself, to make me think such thoughts redeem.
The souls that long ago worked this land,
that persist in death-in-life, leapt into
this stone basin, then floated, eyes shut, through
the inlet toward the Potomac. So stand
here, close your eyes and see: on the river,
that vast primeval beast, their pulses shimmer.

Oak

I had to clear a fallen tree where it lay
across the creek, and five hours passed before
I'd halved, quartered, begun to log the thing,
scrabbling through the mud, cutting out the dense
primeval rot of parasitic creepers,
burning them, digging out the taproot,
heartroot, and the rest—before tossing down
the hole a handful of acorns in hope.
That oak stood proud for over a century
then came down, for no reason I could see.
That night at the doorway of my shack, I stood,
between creekwater sips, watching light drain
out of the sky, and for the briefest instant
shut my eyes and glimpsed the tree where first it grew—
strong, broad, majestic, from the realm of song,
a hundred and twenty years in the leafing,
attended by bluebirds, juncos, finches,
cardinals, flickers, titmice, chickadees,
goldfinches, as made me lose all thought
of who or what or where I was, and could
have lost myself forever there.

Psychic Bobcat

He was there when I glanced up—survivor
of a time long distant when the earth, in
her first spring, sustained countless diverse
creatures unseen since: the Megalodon,

Smilodon, the Troodon, the Quagga,
Moa and Titanoboa. His trance
declared him vortex of disorder
embodied in that zero-bullshit stance.

There he was, eyes pinned on Dakota, primed
to disconnect and dismantle, his
special skill to execute in moments, blind,
with deadly fluency of itamae's

blade, and far less fuss. "What is it, digger?"
(I thought he said.) "I'm the hi-def beastlord
of Gotham, and no city slicker
can stop me offing and chomping his adored

pit-bull. This is my backyard, pussy ass!
and you're a tourist. So have fun, porch monkey,
and when you're done spying on weeds and grass,
get back to Georgetown!" Well, I was hungry

and maybe this was some juice-driven daymare,
I don't know, but when I opened my eyes, glanced
upriver and far off saw him on the flood,
he turned and held me with his eyes, his stance

assured, to tell me, with a blink and a nod,
he'd be back this way one of these fine
September days, swathed in goldenrod,
blazing star and jewelweed, to find

us resting quietly in the sun when,
should chance allow, he'd enjoy our company
all at once and in high style. Then again,
he could just make it quick and perfunctory.

Sometimes on these long, dry summer days
I suspect we're not alone and seize
my cane and peer into the heat-haze
on the creek, but nothing's in the breeze.

And I go on, not doubting he'll
be victor in the end: time's his friend.
He'll dine off the spoil of fishermen's creels
long after my soul has been condemned.

Healing Blue

Mní wičhóni. (Water is life.)

To the tribe these waters were "healing blue"
for their curative powers. Thirty miles
due north, an underground spring feeds into
Dream Lake, round the subterranean isles
of Luray, before pouring its virtue
into the creek that cuts through ravines
in this ancient forest. The tribe knew
water moved in time with the submarine
pulse of its own life. "It dreams in emotions
of when there'll be nothing but itself, swelling,
a time when ocean combines with ocean,
sea with sea." And from it they drank, willing
its power to redeem, restore, return
all the world saw fit to murder, damn and burn.

Posse of Terror

The moon was bright, a sylvan scene,
and the grizzled Major roared through
it with his *infernal machine*—

that greedy unstable crew
of rapists, killers, deserters,
whackjob malcontents, drunks, and slew

of one-eyed, one-legged predators
from the War-that-was, an unchecked
army of righteous creditors

hand-picked by God—posse elect—
to claim what the redskin savage
owed. Eight and fifty strong, they leapt

into the creek, set to ravage
that native clan who had no thought
this might not be an average

day—with their children being taught
to fish, women preparing food,
men checking what their traps had caught

that night, or so we may conclude.
For we've no evidence to say
what happened here within this wood.

The tribe, they must have gone away
the local people said, though none
knew when or why or on which day

they might have hit the trail. The sun
continued shining and the rain
still poured upon that slope, though none

returned to see the place again.
I sometimes think of how, on some
calm and tranquil night, moonlight stains

the creek with whiteness; so thoughts spun
of soothing wish-fulfilment can
obscure what we've become.

The beast is father of the man.

Cleansed

They summered out here on the riverside—
women in the fields, the men catching fish,
children playing by the weir. And I wish
that day had never come. From far, astride
their horses, they watched in shadow while sun
beamed down, unmoved. And today, unchanged,
sky and river are again engaged
in mutual admiration, while each one
of the ancient oaks admires their graces
in the water, just as when the men arrived.
But this is guesswork, for they contrived
to deny it all and dismiss such places
from history, lest the vengeful dead
rise up, possess our minds and drive us mad.

Sylvan Philosopher

We sat for hours and watched the vastness flow:
the Potomac led us to its banks that day—
I felt its pulse inside my head, Dakota too,
possessing all that it could touch. When done,
she took me home down unknown ways,
and we entered a clearing where she stopped.
I peered into darkness but saw nothing
while the murmur of the forest intensified;
starlight blue, glint of fur, breath indrawn—fox.
Dakota still, calm, as he drew closer.
That's when I thought I heard the voice.
"Trees recall the time before our time,
remember the tribes that farmed this soil,
that walk here still. They've seen it all—sundance
round the cottonwood, healing rites, vision quests,
every ritual after death." Fox emerged
into sight and Dakota sank to the ground;
this was he that stole the gift of fire from heaven.
     In former days, the tribe respected
fox's powers, treated him as honored guest—
more than beast, only slightly less than god.
So when the shaman saw the world aflame,
including elders, children, mothers, they sought him.
He sniffed the air and shut his eyes and thought—
all things passed through air—and soon he had them,
five short miles to the north—the Leesburg raiders
as they called themselves—he saw them clear,
their lust for gold, hunger for land, loathing
of redskins, desire to butcher whoever

they found, like their cousins in Turner Falls, Bear
River, Skull Creek, Massapequa, and
Sacramento River. That evening,
on the point of sundown, the raiders
descended on that pool of greenness
in the forest, seeking males, females,
infants and their soft, silky, innocent
blood—but on arrival saw nothing other
than glowing flakes, embers, ashy zephyrs
and the blood-red sky as the sun sank low
behind a mountain. Then one, a trusted voice—
"This place is proper cursed." These men—
unsophisticated, rural, farming folk—
believed in portents, omens, shooting stars,
and land was tainted if the right man said
the word. Each glanced at the next, turned for home.
Except one, Lieutenant Grosbeek, paused,
for somewhere outside his range of vision,
the dim-seen image of fox and some thought
but half-formed, he knew not what. And then
he looked round and headed for Leesburg.
What happened to the raiders I can't tell,
but they weren't seen again.
                              Tonight, on my porch,
Fox partakes of stew and pieces of jerk chicken;
a sociable diner, he loves these evenings
with me and Dakota. More than beast,
only slightly less than god, he recounts
tales five centuries old of the deities
he has come to know—Humwawa, Pazuzu—
not doubting I will understand, though I do not.
Then, distracted, he snaps at the skydiving

mosquitoes round about his ears and growls.
He's our philosopher, for he knows both
what we are, and why. And other things that
make no sense to me.

Roof Repair

Sealing this wooden roof with tar, a yearly
job, I wipe my brow. The tribe on this
hardscrabble slope made Arcadian bliss,
but how? Both Dakota and I nearly
froze last winter, while in summer we bake.
The cabin's centuries old, and I feel
obliged to patch its wounds and conceal
its scratches against whatever shocks might take
it down. If you were to say I was wasting
my time, I might say maybe so. But how
is that different from anything now
and here? And isn't the hastening
moment all we have until, at last,
the present is wrenched untimely from our grasp?

Learn-not-to-be

Back from nowhere after the cold—New Jersey Tea,
golden seal, mayapple, pipsissewa, bloodroot
and countless well-established things, recruits
pressed into service to set us free

from sickness. The cynic in me thinks, please,
what's the herbal cure for death? Laughing,
I open the cabin door, catching
a voice from nowhere—Learn-not-to-be.

Prospect

Halfway down the choked trail that runs
to the mailbox, Dakota halted. Glancing
her way, I nearly missed it: speaking in tongues,
flying at lightning speed, some dancing
forest leshy crossed our path, followed by
streaks of red-gray barking, yelping—fox
in pursuit, set to catch a mind's-eye
vision in a field of wild blue phlox.
No end to the prospect that, for a moment,
opened in half-darkness that space in which
we quest for something like atonement.
But when we come back it's black as pitch:
too late for thoughts of grace or closure—
shut your eyes and let the black take over.

Bushcraft

Heartrot was eating the life of the tree.
Its flesh had gone soft; sticky ooze covered
the bark. If I didn't take an ax to it,
it would fall. To the tribe, trees were home to
spirits good and bad, released by felling.
But that's not why I stood there, ax in hand:
I'd lain here, in the clearing, several times,
imagining the day when, enjoying
the clarity and freshness of the brisk
November air, I'd expire *al fresco*.
Perhaps, as consciousness receded,
I'd be submerged among hermaphrodites
of earth—sightless wrigglesworths staking
their claim, entering lips, earholes, eyes, nostrils,
trailing clouds of mucus—or aware instead
of beasts of the bush, furred and feathered,
gnawing skin and organs, veins and guts and
gristle of the John Doe that was me, now
chewed and churned and broken down so giving me
purpose anew—more, some might say, than in
life. I placed my hand on the tree's wide trunk,
raised my ax and swung
embedding that blade in the tree's white flesh.

Reliquary

"They went south for sure," said honest Ed,
"took their livestock south on Georgetown Pike."
"But their two hounds," I said, "—maimed, blinded,
found in the woods; charred bones; heads on spikes

down by the creek." He knew nothing of that
though old man Mackail claimed all ten acres
and swore he'd fight like a flaming wildcat
to hold them. A week later, said neighbors,

he burned down most of the trees on the plot
to turn into fields. You couldn't cross
Mackail and his three boys; they always got
what they desired. And then, what loss

if the brutes had gone? They'd be forgotten.
There was no witness that saw what transpired,
so if that land-claim was misbegotten
none could judge—but then, none enquired.

None enquired and none enquired and soon
it was as if they had never been,
until today, this glorious afternoon—
here, where they wintered out, this sylvan scene,

this corner of the ancient wood untouched
by Mackail, where even now I find black
snakeroot, eastern redbud, columbine just
by the creek, while up the slope, near the shack,

flowering dogwood, witch hazel, turtlehead,
once used as medicines by the tribe,
growing here in profusion: living things spread
before me, traces of those blameless lives.

Of the Creek

The creek is the agent of transformation;
I've seen the southern sprite emerge from it,
the snake doctor and the water witch—
these are the agents of revelation.
They promise freedom from anxiety-fire
rampaging through the mind, forgiveness
of all that pursues us through the stillness
of the silence of the night. So inspired,
I wade slowly through the creek, compelled
to surrender to the otherworld, hoping
the water will possess me, floating
me out to the river—and then ask myself,
"Came I to the creek that I might pray
or am I here to wash my sins away?"

Constellation

Where these four walls meet the cabin floor
I plant these quartz stones taken from the creek.
I began collecting because I adore
      their shade of palest pink,

their smoothness, roundness, wrought by water, grit
and all the years I wasn't here; though now
I sense that something else compels my spirit.
      The Cherokee endow

the crystal with energy; led by them,
I gather stones I hope will form a shield,
my guardian cobra with gorgeous gem
      pulsing in its head, sealed

within the rock. And in the depths of night
they appear to glow as if reminded
of deep space—the rhapsodies of light,
      wise matter, excited,

turning spirals in frozen darkness,
conscious of a species of ecstasy
felt by bodies possessed of the calmness
      of their sweet destiny.

The Expired

Before the sun rises, darkness becomes
fragile; nothing on the hillside seems quite
as it should, it's weak and prone to succumb
to all that shall lay waste the visions of night.
When it comes, light is blinding, and the dead
who stood in the shades, in my thoughts, are no more.
But grief's not easily put aside;
it brings back the dead who, till crack of dawn,
besiege us in sleep, and won't lie down
or go away, preferring to fill our dream
and waking lives. They loiter in some lounge
for the deceased, waiting to be redeemed.
Darkness fosters grieving and sadness
out of which come neurosis and madness.

Tears

Ice becoming water trickling down the hill—
I could wish to see the landscape each day
run with tears, that in devotion it will
nourish its pieties, for it knows how clay
makes war on clay, fruit of centuries
of witness even in this sheltered valley.
It's as if we see the tension ease—
on either side the waters carry
grief and thoughts of all that happened here
away. Yet as we walk down to the stream
we're reminded grief can never disappear,
grows into us, part of all we see and seem.
Cry as you will but when the last tear is shed
a moment's thought can summon back the dead.

Death of the Angel

Branches slamming the window panes,
darkness killing the light. Those sleepless hours
stretched out although I tried to shut my eyes,
listening to my pounding heart. By four
the weather had calmed, though the sky was
black as tar. At such times, thought the tribe,
restless spirits passed through the night,
besought their place in this and other worlds
in strange and stranger forms. Still I couldn't
sleep and after a while heard Dakota
at the door that she might venture forth.
"What's up?" I asked; she cocked her head.
I unlatched the door and out she raced:
when I caught her up she was at the foot
of the hill facing an adult cottonmouth
risen two feet high, glaring down on her.
Two heads it had—*two*—as one were one too few.
My impulse was to shoot them all the way
to Sevastopol. "You see some beast",
my daddy used to say, "you *kill it*, is that clear?"
Rather than fight, Dakota placed her muzzle
on the ground; in turn the snake relaxed its pose,
one snakehead fixed on me while the other
hovered at Dakota's ear, delivering
admonishment from another world.
Then both heads turned as one, and in my skull
I heard a female voice—"Careful. Killing
a snake is perilous." And in that moment
it seemed to me the voice was a third mind

combo—Dakota, snake, me, in a single
harmonized utterance. The serpent turned,
slithered toward the creek and, at the edge,
both heads glanced back at us—o creature from the
world before the flood, were you sister of
Jörmungandr, child of Loki and the giantess
Angrboða? Why did I not bid you
speak of what you know of the cosmos, man,
and where we're going? Too late, too late!
Slowly, it entered the water and sank
till its heads were all we could see, then
disappeared. I followed Dakota to
the edge of the creek and stared—no trace,
just the water flowing on its way.
With shame it occurred to me I had been
at the center of a cosmic labyrinth
without knowing it. I was a fool.

    Winter sprang upon us; one day I saw
ice pellets almost static in mid-air,
wondered at their meaning. Then one night in
December, Dakota at the door again,
to be let into the early morning air.
I threw it open and she raced past me,
heading for the creek. I found her sitting
with remnants of a single snake—fresh gutted,
two heads bitten to pieces, bloodied, on
the ground. Above us, a family of
crows rattling, screeching, whose breakfast we had
interrupted. I glanced at shreds and ends
of that bright ophidian creature we'd
encountered months before—at which the crows
swooped down and swiped what scraps remained, no sooner

on the forest floor than back up in the trees.
Their victim's blood and bones were scattered in
the grass to be washed away by tears
of angels in the pre-dawn air. I turned
back to the shack with Dakota. In days
following I saw tumors form on trees,
raccoons eating squirrels, and betimes,
on cusp of day, out the edge of the
corner of my eye, sensed that two-headed
serpent, in all the beauty it once had,
somewhere close by, watching me.

Gale Force

Gales bowl in off the mid-Atlantic,
drunk with power, locked out of this shack
by invisible force-lines, geomantic
figures laid down by bibliomaniac
strategies of stacking and shelving. Cyclonic
winds ram the forest, felling trees dying
or dead, and shelter in some chthonic
realm seems for now a fortifying
choice, dark though it be, lonely and cold.
When the wind dies down I step outside
to check nearby trees for signs their foothold
remains secure. Though I have to confide,
on issues like this you must be precisional:
hold on life can be mighty provisional.

Deliriant

I'd been thinning out the hawthorns and greenbriers
out on the slope and now lay in the sun
on the porch, and there, on the frontiers
of conscious thought, for an instant thought I'd outrun
all that was finite to become eight feet tall
ditchweed, madapple, devil's snare, locoweed—
swaying slowly in the breeze, in thrall
to sphinx-moth larvae crazy to feed
on my leaves till they explode in flight,
bearing riddles of ancient renown
across the southern states' days and nights,
there to baffle and bruise, confuse and confound,
as they have done since white men came,
when perfection fell to chaos, never the same.

Insectisonic

Dark-timbred, metallic-toned, katydids,
crickets, break out the night—radiant waves
of stridulated heat filling woods, caves
and clearings with hot-wired, massing plasmids

fixated on seduction. From the base
of my spine weightlessness lifts my heels, jerks from
the top of the head: their unified wing-strum
carries me through reaches of deep space

and I could remain forever there
beyond the moon's dark side, blackness of black,
without thought or speech, to be taken back
to the state of absence or reverie, where

the invisible, unnoticed, flashes
through our eyes, ballast floats upward, and things,
words and images, as if they had wings,
float round and over the underpasses

of the somnolent mind—though, when I blink,
I'm back on the sheltered slope of this hill,
embraced by your buzz-saw symphony till
those long-legged leapers begin to think

this the hour for love and death and revelry
and cease as one, behind them leaving air ravished
by roused night-burring—harmonies lavished
on the night's cold indifference and me.

Photuris

And then the hour when the fireflies come;
dazzling angels in the twilight shimmer
inviting males to join them for dinner,
but first beneath the Japanese plum
a rhumba or mambo or a tango
or salsa, a Latin trick to tighten
her grip and compel his mood to ripen
for the finale—played *sforzando*.
Those hapless males, could they but speak, would say
"What do I here, in nature's abattoir
which never closes?" Your glistering star,
dear Sir, doomed you to finish things this way!
Oh the thousand thousand flickering fires;
nothing endures, everything dies.

Orthoptera Motet

Two in the morning, someone starts; seconds
later they're in the groove, a symphony,
fizzling, and something more—an epiphany,
deafening, drowning me from all directions.

Possess, embrace me, let me carouse in
your glittering world of noise; fold me into
your night-time chorale, let me construe
the infinite palace of your rolling

thunder. Your voices fill this broken world,
infuse its shattered pieces, as if your
coruscations could redeem and restore
to them their proper dignity, conserved

and filled with life. So insects confound,
disincarnate me now, let me surrender
shape, self, identity, to your splendor,
you, your roar, and a place in the sound.

Etiology

Confined to this room while rain hammers down
I see mud breathed into life, greenness
uprisen at mid-noon; the feral ground
pulsing with stones shivered by their own genius,
underworld warriors with scores to settle
storming through this primeval forest;
trees shudder, shake in elemental
terror as they spring from earth caressed
by vivifying waters of the air.
Behold this fallen Eden as dreamscape
of rapacious and living blood, where
sons butcher their fathers and rape
their mothers—endless repeating swordplay,
redemption further and further away.

Skin

Dakota dragged something from a pile
of leaves against the cabin wall: graceful,
translucent, filigree snakesuit. So I
took it inside, laid it on a table.

"Matter's what changes—nothing else!" Voices
melt from the treetops when you're alone
in the forest. There were few choices;
I decided to bury it under the stone

just outside the cabin door. That was two
months gone. Each day the voice returns
to bewail its fate—forcibly subdued,
hidden from light, for freedom it yearns

yet remains out of sight, though in my mind,
lamenting restraint. O trance-traveler,
whirled by hurricanes out of your rhyme,
stay—safe from entropy, time's unraveller.

Fired Up

Ruthless hot the angry August sun glares
down upon the slope. Nothing moves. My
dog sleeps in a pool of light while I stare
at a gap in the outer wall which I
will have to fill. Though not right now. With luck
I can ignore it till the weather cools.
This is the unforgiving rut I'm stuck
within—a heat-induced inertia rules.
Yet this inaction, I begin to think,
is that to which all human business tends,
for everything resolves as rest: a blink,
and what once was living finds that end.
Whatever is, is burning up—you, me;
to burn to ash is what it is to be.

Copperhead Rendition

Out the dusklands of silent slumber a bark—
Dakota. We'd fallen asleep before
the fire that dark November evening
after our journey through the forest and back.
I leaned forward to comfort her, but found
her wide-eyed, rigid, trembling—and only
when I turned did I see why. Our visitor
calm, watchful, on the rug, staring at me
with yellow-black eyes, blank and pitiless
as the sun. To the tribe he'd been a god
forged at core of the earth. They etched
his likeness into their bodies, daubed it
on their shrines, traced it in the sky at midnight,
embedded it in their origin myth:
eastern copperhead, earth-brown, earth-golden.
As I stared, his tongue flickered out and in,
and from somewhere in my skull a voice said,
"Transfer to Leviathan". I knew what to do;
found a box, forced back its lips, placed its
mouth before him—a blink, and he entered
the void. I closed it, picked it up and stepped
into the cold. All was darkness-drenched yet
the palest light came bleeding through the clouds.
I sprinted down the slope, slithered down it,
impelled by some strange rhythm in the brain
toward the fury of the Potomac—
waters seething at thought of being lost
forever in the boiling Chesapeake.
Carefully, I set down the box, pulled open

the flaps and stood well back. Snake emerged slow,
made his way toward those angry waters,
bridge to unlife, shrill with traffic of angels
and the dead. And how I marveled at the
glistering scales, for he was royalty
even in darkness on the quaggy banks of
this vast river. Had he come from Eden?,
I wondered. "You think of Paradise lost,"
said a voice within, "yet the dream, the dream
is everywhere." Even by faint moonlight
I could see his tongue, knew he was bidding farewell,
when of a sudden his eyelids shut and
he immersed himself in the living dark
of that ancient beast, Old Potomac.
And there we stood listening—sound as soothing
as to the first that walked these shady banks.
I picked up a small, round, quartzite pebble
which had touched his coils, as token of what
we'd seen, returned to the cabin. At the fire now,
as the moon showers these woods with light,
I'd have to say he remains a visitor,
his shape cut into sills, doorframes, floorboards:
depicting him has become an obsession
for me. You see, he owns this place, was present
long before we came, and will be many years
after we are gone. Which may be why I
sometimes sense him right behind me, watching,
waiting, poised to speak.

Succession

"By countless empires were we preceded
and in our turn will we be succeeded."

So it runs; yet as I stepped out
of the cabin that morning after days
of continual rain, I had no doubt
there was worse in store. Because we've always
nursed the cataclysm as the ultimate
disaster—who's to say when it might come?
I walked down to the creek, brought its luculent
waters to my face, and it was as if some
lease on life had been renewed, a feeling
good enough to wipe away the memory
of these last days, as well as any meaning
I might attach to them in reverie.
A little sunlight upon the scene
can prompt the mind to forget what it conceives.

Silver Dollar

I found a silver dollar in the dirt
minted the year of Posse Comitatus—
the year that, having lost their ardor
for the redskins, the white folk took their spacious
acreage saying, "The savages, the entire
troop, have hit the Pittsburgh trail." Days before,
they'd turned these woods into slaughterhouse and pyre
though, without a word, all of Langley swore
to bite its tongue and cast its gaze on the ground.
After all, the redskins had no legal right
to that huge tract of land; them with their coonhounds
were outlaws, a source of illness, blight.
The self-judging mind is prone to laxity
when it's confronted by reality.

(Posse Comitatus Act, enacted 1878)

Love Story

When Death swung by, so I assumed,
he'd be looking for me, and to him I'd say:

"Howdy amigo, what took you so long?"
But all these years have slipped lately by and

I'd say either you, my love, or me, could
be next on his list. Mallet to the skull,

cheese knife to the heart, mattock to the neck:
these, my petal, might be acts of love from me

to you, passionate as that night I first
made love to you, forcing your neck back hard

to the wall, slapping your face over and
over—so I know you know how true love feels.

Brain-rot, cancer-rot, sugarbetes, stroke:
whichever plague might come, I'll force you to
the wall, pull your jaws apart, give you the cure—

love, sweet love, on the blade of a billhook.

How It Is

You're struggling one hot afternoon to uproot
a thicket of wild, self-seeded thorny
olives when you have that sudden, acute
tingling in the brain because it's stormy
in the end-zone: let your spade descend
silently to earth, then you watch as the ground
slams you like an unhinged door. You're condemned.
You wanted to speak, say something profound,
go with dignity, surrounded
by grandchildren—not like this, in this cold
autumnal landscape, at dusk, confounded,
tearful, terrified, guilt-racked, unconsoled.
But it's too late: you're inert and dumb,
waiting to be whatever you'll become.

Wake

"Dead, we become the lumber of the world." (Rochester)

Each morning they come to truffle and pike and poke;
sometimes, if I'm on the porch, Kong sits under that tree
before me, extending his tongue: high devotee
of the ministry of darkness, he coos and croaks

as he takes my measure, sniffing out what he thinks might
best slay me—big mac brain-bleed, spinning wheel of death,
myocardial infarction, shortness of breath.
He smacks his lips. He sees me as Meatball Delight

with garlic butter gravy, followed by helpings of gourmet
gelato. So there's me, flat on my back (code blue)
while Kong rounds up the clan—Basil, Eve, Lulu,
Zelda, Chopper and Skewers—as if in Café

Deux Magots, or guests at some Caribbean resort—
he musters them then they go frenzilicious
over my corpse. To them all's nutritious
from snout to flipper, from import to export,

sex appeal to beau ideal, till a smattering
of bones is all that remains of that decadent blow-out
al fresco. Then, like gods, they take to the air, seed the clouds
with dyspeptication, trademark scattering

out the cargo flap. What was once us
begins to combust just as soon as we're born
until, by the end, we're cold and outworn,
sublimed by life into gristle and dust.

In the Groove

Old as hellflame, treefrogs awaken high
in their aerial towers, full of rage
to flourish, old as glacial rocks that lie
at my feet. They shake the forest, uncage
that chirruping bark that simmers from here to
downtown Shepherdstown. I've felt it since
before I was born, something I knew
in my mother's womb with power to evince
our shared origins in that prehistoric
age of slaughter and survival. Their throb,
their visceral croak, is a euphoric,
a tribal chant that tells me where I'm from:
whenever the frogs possess me with rhythm
I'm remade by their musical vision.

Echoes

Like one of those forests, deep in darkness,
where in the early nineties we partied
with hundreds of others under starless
skies, afterward turned to each other, started
walking to the woods, unable to see
each others' faces so kissed and touched
the more intensely, that now when we
think in this dark place tonight or tomorrow
might bring our end, we have memories
of that campsite long ago. Time reduces
as the past thrives, unfolding its emperies
in the landscape of the mind. Time produces
echoes, past and present seeming synchronous—
vain thoughts, born of human wishfulness.

Trail

Water over stone was all I heard that night
as if earth sought the healing power it knew
was locked in that mad chatter. And it's true
    I woke up feeling almost right,

no longer fearful of the day to come.
But the sickness in the earth beneath me,
its trauma at witness, has slowly seeped
    through this landscape which now succumbs

to that force that causes walls to fail
and cells to die. It chants, "We wanted night
to cover our deeds before the daylight
    came, but we left a trail:

they'll hunt us down, they'll run us down
and string us up, we'll hang here until next spring
while the devil pecks our innards out
    and his minions make us sing."

Homer

The head swung in darkness, eye-bolted
to a chain wrapped round a branch, blue tongue
wailing dirges of bitter loss jolted
from the fading ghost of consciousness, strung

to the oldest melodies deep-buried in
primeval thud of brain and phlegm. They thwacked
and blinded it with stones and sticks, bade it sing
of godlessness, fights and foulness old, quacked

out and out, black into air—songs conceived
by long dead autochthonous beings
whose daughters consorted, so it's believed,
with seraphim, pursued gross unwreathings

with daemons of air, lords of unreason,
lords of panic, lords of wrath. With each bite
of the stick that foul thing retched, seized on
an utterance, a posture, a slight,

sicked it to light with vile slobber-spasming,
bestial, eyes-bulging, screeches of fear,
as it saw in daymare the phantasming
of battle known to a sick musketeer.

One wrought its croaks into verses, one jabbed
a piss-rag in its gobhole, another
held a blade which she now and then stabbed
what were once its ears; lover by lover

they sat down beside it, hungry to imbibe
oracular visions of the gore-drenched young,
while an aged woman, half-deaf, transcribed
each metered line on a tablet of dung.

Purveyor of furious conflict,
it told of man pining for his quarry
that he might strike, spike, slice, and with strict
discipline resect and dice, each blade-flurry

like a bed of kisses till, stunned, he sees
nothing holds the brains inside its head.
Such tales retold and told again much pleased
the crowds that later sought the dark, contented.

Hours after this excess of jabbering
in the coldness and solitude and blankness
of night, the thing could not stop blabbering,
though now quite distinctly, as in dankness

and misery it needed to declare
the sacred beauty of nature, the stunned
pain of loss, and the predicted day to come—
hymns beyond imagining of anyone,

harmonized with breezes of the night,
a simmering medley, a gift conferred,
flung at the sleeping world with all its might
though not thought of, unreported and unheard.

Early Morning

Before the sun comes up, the light is flat
and weak; nothing looks quite as it should—
provisional, as if trees within this wood
were changed, made less substantial, almost glad
no more to be oppressed by light. The dead
wander as they will, pursuing
their affairs (or someone else's), renewing
their love of earth before the dark is fled
and with it, possibility. That's why
I walk out when it gets like this—to lose
myself among those ghosts whose
company makes me feel most alive,
and most of all, to know thereby
how to prepare for when I die.

Badass

Tiger mosquitoes everywhere down the creek.
We followed the restless, uncoiling river
all the way out to the Falls, sometime trading-
post of Chief Powhatan, and took our ease
among pignut hickory and chestnut
oak that throng what once was the ancient riverbed.
The dead were everywhere in twos and threes;
after a while I dozed away the afternoon,
and so did Dakota. Too soon, too soon,
day slipped past us, dusk fell sudden into night.
We fled home down wooded trails—Dakota
leading, glancing back, ensuring I was
safe until, unknowing, we entered the
swampy microclimate by the creek,
where the denizenry were addicted
to stabbing, burning, biting, stinging—
rabid for meatstick charcuterie,
driven hump-mad by relentless heat.
Dakota's trailfinding nose kept us close
to the chatter of water over stone but
almost in sight of our cabin, by a
massive beech-tree, I was struck by blue-light
streaks of bark-bound *scincidae* etching air
in azure pinstripes—sharp as a high-power
laser beamline—o mercury eyes with
untold depths—shaman, magician, trickster—
love-child of iguana, raptor, monitor,
yea, prelapsarian *scincomorpha*.
Can I be the first that yearned to quiz them

about the lamented Nyasasaurus,
the second snowball Earth, giants, the deluge,
plagues of Egypt or, more usefully,
when our world will come to grief? I might have
stayed forever there, in that dream-chamber,
listening to them speak of this "dark place"
where evil possessed even those determined
to do right. But I was rattled by whirling
fleets of yellowjackets, chorus of treefrogs,
crickets, katydids warning of stormquakes
spiraling out of nowhere, tracing their
chaotic path northwards from somewhere south-
east of Tampa Bay. And those scrounge lizards
kept their poker faces, calmly scoring
gnats on the nips of their tongues as they squared
up to the fuckwave, badass gullywasher,
no-shit cyclone headed our way, which they'd
calmly observe as it roiled the Potomac,
knocked out infirm trees and zeroed some pricey
jammers—Mercs, Jags, Beamers and, if lucky,
a Lambo in that memorable shade,
Bianco Icarus—before shimmying
off the dancefloor into the grey wastes of
the Atlantic. Dakota whined; she knew
what was coming, led me back to the cabin.
I locked the door in time to watch bullying,
pummeling winds fight free of trees that thrashed,
writhed, screamed: zag of lightning, an approaching roar,
but my mind reverted to the five-line skink,
tox as fuck that placid sadhu among
the beechen green and shadows numberless—
cold-blooded priest at the fire-ceremony.

At length Dakota slept and so did I,
to dream of that endless counterclockwise
odyssey, whirling dervishes, falling
angels, the landscape of Mars, dogs playing
poker, the gravedigger in *Hamlet*,
tribesmen long dissolved in the gritstone moorlands
of Staffordshire who nursed the terminal
inflection as Milton did in Satan's
list of every class of angel—"Thrones,
Dominations, Princedoms, Virtues, Powers."

Dream-Beasts

Beasts old as the world pelting through underbrush—
dream-beasts at heart of the place's memory
of times long distant. They pass rapidly
unseen down the creek and into the crush
of riverwater, then out out into
future time—and I ask what is that world
they call home, where they live, or are they whirled
through the zones, not to settle somewhere new?
Witnesses to ruins of empire and
bloodiest war, they know how far we'll go,
and in this valley how brutal the blow
that swept the tribe from their ancestral land.
If only they weren't a thought in my head
but a voice for the forgotten and dead.

Stay

The beech behind the cabin was sick: I
had to down it lest, come the next hard storm,
me and Dakota inside, it die

and fall. I roped the trunk one breezy, warm
September day, lashed it to boulders, stakes
in hope of keeping it clear of harm

that it might fall *up* the hill, not erase
me and my shack. I could have felled it then
but something withheld me I couldn't trace,

an instinctive feeling, strangely intense:
Stay, it said, put down your saw instead.
And instead of cutting I had to dispense

with my tools like one in dream, turn my head
to other things and let the tree alone.
Since that time twelve years nine months are fled

and the tree stands proudly on this limestone
slope, witness to all by which the first tribes
were harassed, stripped of land and overthrown.

Time Suck

In under a minute, day becomes night
when in darkness I doze in this chair
among night-creatures, all out of sight,
who like passing close to me when they dare.
All the nights left to me I'd spend this way
if I could, or end up filled with regret;
but I have to wonder how many remain
till I leave this forest. Time was yet
a friend to me when I first arrived—seemed
slow to move or not at all. Then the years
shot past like days, and decades steamed
out of sight, and time's up soon, or so I hear.
Time doesn't enlarge, instead it teases—
it will starve you just as it damn well pleases.

Last Will

Lay me at the shore of Potomac's flood,
that swelling flood at the edge of the world;
let me sink in alluvial mud,
       in its darkness enfurled.

Bind me in a shroud of dirt, cover my eyes
with a poultice of clay, lay me down
in leafscorch, humus, that the drifting skies
       pass over this mound.

Lay me naked on this slope where the tribe
once laid their dead; let vultures take my brains,
the bobcat my bones; let no shred survive,
       no bones, no bones, no bones.

Articulate Soil

Living their journey through perpetual night,
that family of trees on the valley bottom
marks where, in deepening gloom of twilight,
they embodied rites passed down in solemn
thought preserved since elder-time. Standing there,
eyes shut, an instant pulls me through their chants—
untethered, loose, dancing in nocturnal air
above my head, skyward rising in dance
designed to invoke the dead. But I blink
back to native land, knowing those who once dwelt here
ash, dead embers strewn along this creek,
this place of sighs, of grief, unfettered tears,
that speaks tonight of innocence and blame—
a killing field in all but name.

Snakeland

Trees and bushes running down this hill
possess a darkly glowing intensity
that speaks to me of the dominant will
of the Eastern Copperhead snake. Yet he
remains invisible, though known to tribal
ancestors, shy of human treachery,
friendly only with those of whom, in some primal
manner, he can dream. Snakehides, for their leathery
texture, once were slung over these branches, by those
to whom serpent was a delicacy—
but no one in these parts would now compose
dinner round snakemeat. With elegancy
do the copperheads perform their dances on these clods,
knowing themselves mythic creatures, gods.

Arrowhead

Dakota and I pursued the creek to
the ravine; it runs westward all the way
through the foothills of "blue-mist-land". The day
was bright and our path clear, beyond the view

of any soul—as if we were the last
upon this earth. Dakota ran along
the stream while I dallied with the throng
of plants I might as well have walked right past.

Brightness filled the air, cottonwood fluff, leaves,
seeds, and for an instant I was a guest
in the realm of spirit, wholly possessed
by forms and colors floating on a breeze:

bloodroot, woodsorrel, Virginia bluebell,
Dutchman's breeches, lizard's tail, wild ginger,
grass of Parnassus, tickseed sunflower,
trout lily, Indian hemp and, tall and still,

center of the stream, noble arrowhead fern,
its fronds so shaped, which indigenous
tribes once used for headache—yes, their kindness;
foods and medicines freely given

to settlers when they came. I tried not to think—
thought that could not take, for images bled
through the retina to closed eyes. "The dead
persist within the hearts of the quick."

Where those words came from I don't know—
something I may once have read. I walked back
with Dakota to our log cabin, sat
in its shade, let the hours pass slow and slow.

The Past

I know this place, I always have, although
I've never been before. What the reason
for this recognition? How could I know
this hillside, regardless of the season?
The many years I spent here, the people
I once knew, I see them in glimpses now
from somewhere long ago, before that upheaval
that downed both friend and foe. Somehow
as I wade along this creek, take me back
to the realm of innocence, that distant time
beyond time, when no one sought or lacked
for anything before the darkness came.
Even as I say it, the place and people
slip out of reach, beyond retrieval.

Leaves

Flaming carmine, burning ochre, blown
a hundred feet or more above the world;
as they flutter down, I can't help but wonder
why should beauty be death's calling card?

Back Country

For Gary Snyder

Dakota and I lose ourselves, yet on we go
along this trail, knowing ourselves more lost
than ever we thought—more so, as we cross
another stream we know we did not know.
Yet there's a *frisson*, a sense of release
at vanishing into untrodden ways:
it's an otherlife, an interior maze,
the life unlived, widescreen redemption, peace.
The thing is, I'm trying not to break
the spell, stay this side of the unknown,
but my luck can't hold, my cover's blown,
I'm clenching eyes tight shut lest I awake.
What's familiar lacks intensity;
the unknown sharpens everything I see.

Arboreal Memory

That night the sleepless hours stretched out I shut
my eyes, listening to the hillside,
letting it course through my head until they
came to view—parents, daughters, sons, together

once more. What need of words; sobs and tears were
enough for the dead to pay their respects
to the dead, intensity of feeling
having brought them, just for a second, to

the slope on which their lives had long ago
been lived. And so on these meandering
summer afternoons, when Dakota and
I doze in the heat, oh then if my mind

is idle and thoughtless, I might conceive
them here again—embracing, weeping,
kissing, the dead reclaiming those they loved,
just an instant, in this vacant breeze.

The Cure

He patiently explained, as to a child,
    my only hope—to turn into
    an oak: I agreed, drank the brew.
He cut two longitudinal, hand-styled

shapes, almost serpentine, feet to head, whirred
    through me then slowly inserted
    beautifully crafted inverted
wooden slivers in the wounds, subtly curved,

pushing down through the skull, deep down, into
    the trunk, one after the next, next
    after the other, all direct
through the top of the head, again through

and through again, again, till the body
    was toe to top, sole to crown,
    wood upon wood, all the way down
to the ground, and slender, searching, knotty,

through earthen floor at side of the creek—down,
    down further, into dark soil; fed
    from the husk of the world spread
the wood, deeper tended, to the profound

black, into the bones and ash of the dead.

Survivor

She returns—child on an old dirt track
beneath a parade of beeches and oaks.
"Where's your home?" I want to say, "Your folks?"
But she doesn't know me and won't look back,

last of those who for centuries past
farmed, managed and lived on this land. She treads
the path to the turnpike beyond, threads
her way to the dreamscape vast—

coming and going as night succeeds day,
from land to land, from pole to pole,
survivor of that part of the soul
that knows sin and damnation, and the way

to dusty death. And though she has now gone
from here, this is her place, and her peoples',
regardless of the bloody upheavals
upon these slopes on which she long ago was born.

Conviction

The tribe confronts me as they wait for men
they know will make an end of them; they stand
before me in the woods on the land
where they grew up, which they vowed to defend—
the debt they owe this holy place, the last
thing they must do, the act that will bring their
history to its close. And no pair
of eyes lack hope, nor a face its upcast
glow; and how I envy such conviction—
the belief the world will live, secured
by otherworldly powers, and as reward
be permanent, past and future vision.
"Your people are lost. Although they try,
they don't know how to live or die."

Melville's Crossing

Tuesday April 12, 1864

Snaking north into the bloodlands
of rebel-held northern Virginia,
the Potomac led the platoon far from
the sight of the Capitol's new dome.
In midst of Civil War, Herman Melville
journeyed through an enemy state in search of
his cousin Henry, maybe dead, but said
to be among Union troops. Fort by fort,
there'd been little to see till they reached the
badlands of Georgetown Pike, where all them
Billy Bob peckerwoods had been holed up
since velociraptors ruled Mongolia.
These junglelands were cannibal country:
the forest lived by rules stemming from
feudal times, imposed by colonial
landlords, stretching for miles along Potomac's
banks all the way to Leesburg—perfect cover
for Mosby's Raiders. There were ferals living
in these woods, answerable to no one.
A place like this can get you killed,
the platoon leader said, words that Melville
only now began to comprehend. This
was Langley, settlement in the zone of
anarchy. Smoke rose sluggishly from
brutish shacks of wattles, decades old,
visible from the road—obscene dens of
moonshine-makers, squirrel-mongers, trout-smokers,
snakegod worshippers. This territory

was unmapped because cartographers
entered but never emerged; it was thought
they were captured, skinned, deknackered, dismembered
while breathing, then toasted, roasted or simmered
on an open fire. Somewhere in the bush,
a soldier told him, a cook was known to prepare
human breast-meat while the heart was beating still.
He had warned: "Don't stop; don't stare at the hogs"
(people, he meant) "and, whatever you do,
keep moving"… And yet, how could he pass through
here without eyeballing the pigs on this
forsaken track—descendants of the Kentish folk
who'd sailed with Lord Fairfax more than a hundred
and fifty years before? Which made these inbred
turnipheads Fairfax's legacy, with their
gnarled, inked, foul-smelling, sun-beaten bodies,
meagerly-clad in pelts of goat and squirrel;
some were idiots, one was chained to a post,
another was in a cage. They were of the land
forgot by time, and would cast their unwholesome
juices into that fetid puddle from
which would come the genetic cocktail called
America. Half a mile down the trail
he glimpsed a bearded man in a soiled apron,
gripping a bloody carcass by its tail:
their eyes met. The man looked as if he knew him,
what and who he was. Melville saw the cleaver
dripping at his side, averted his gaze.
What abominations lay within these
dwellings? The platoon continued through
ancient glades, up and down hills, small and large,
as they pursued the path laid down a

millennium ago by the indigenous
people. Minutes later it dipped as it
might take them to the Virgilian
underworld, a place he wanted to see—
down and down as far as they could go until
the track leveled out in a pool of sunlight
at a rustic mill. "Mama Swinks's tavern!"
yelled a soldier as they dismounted,
and the entire platoon disappeared inside.
Melville looked about; the mill sat on a creek
that rushed across the trail into the woods
leading to the Potomac, though he was drawn
more by the shade of beeches and oaks
which he knew at a glance to be more than
three centuries old. One in particular—
he touched its bark, inhaled, clenched his eyes
as a shock of light ran through him: men, women,
children whose features were like the Marquesans'
with whom he lived more than twenty years before.
But these were descendants of the first people,
those who crossed the land-bridge from Siberia,
trekked over glaciers to get here.
And they spoke to him, and he could understand
their words as if their tongue were his. They spoke
of the first man and woman, of that fardistant
time when none had eaten
another's flesh or worn its skin or
made it labor, when no disease had struck down
those that lived. And with each breath in the seconds
that passed, he lived lifetimes, saw the births of
generations, died, was born again and
lived again. He was warrior, poet,

shaman, king, and as the centuries rolled
over him, as ages on ages passed
over him, as he lived life after life
in this ancient forest, he knew it would end
but yearned to remain forever there.

Awakening, Melville swayed uncertainly,
holding tight the oak-tree's branch as he slipped
back into that faint echo of an echo
fainter still. He was staring at something
beneath the water of the creek: a small
white stone that radiated light. He reached down
and raised it to his eye. Quartzite, pinky-cream—
worn and worn and worn away by passage
of water and time. He walked to the tavern
to find the platoon long departed.
Glancing one last time into the grove,
he promised to return. In later years
he'd gaze at the stone, recalling the place,
though he knew in his heart he'd never return.
But, he thought, he was one of those natives,
one of the first people of the beechen grove:
the thought was there and then it was gone.
Years later, after his death, his widow
found the stone in his desk with other things,
all worthless, cast them away. It was,
after all, just a stone.

"We are all of us—Anglo-Saxons, Dyaks, and Indians—sprung from
one head, and made in one image. And if we regret this brotherhood
now, we shall be forced to join hands hereafter." (Melville, March 31,
1849)

Afterword

It is believed over 10 million indigenous people were living in the Americas when Europeans discovered the new continent; that had plummeted to 300,000 by 1900. Over the centuries, many means were used to kill them, including the use of bounties, and distribution of smallpox-infected blankets. Today, native Americans remain targets of discrimination and continue to fight for restitution of ancestral lands.

www.ingramcontent.com/pod-product-compliance
Lightning Source LLC
Chambersburg PA
CBHW022200080426
42734CB00006B/523